DOVER · THRIFT · EDITIONS

Hardy's Selected Poems

THOMAS HARDY

DOVER PUBLICATIONS, INC.
New York

DOVER THRIFT EDITIONS

GENERAL EDITOR: STANLEY APPELBAUM
EDITOR OF THIS VOLUME: BOB BLAISDELL

Copyright

Copyright © 1995 by Dover Publications, Inc.
All rights reserved under Pan American and International Copyright Conventions.

Published in Canada by General Publishing Company, Ltd., 30 Lesmill Road, Don Mills, Toronto, Ontario.

Published in the United Kingdom by Constable and Company, Ltd., 3 The Lanchesters, 162–164 Fulham Palace Road, London W6 9ER.

Bibliographical Note

This Dover edition, first published in 1995, is a new selection of poems by Thomas Hardy (all but one of the texts are those of *Collected Poems of Thomas Hardy*, published by Macmillan and Co., Ltd., London, 1919; "The Calf" is from *The Book of Baby Beasts* by Florence Dugdale, published by Frowde, London, 1911). The introductory Note, explanatory footnotes, and Alphabetical Lists of Titles and First Lines have been specially prepared for the present edition.

Library of Congress Cataloging-in-Publication Data

Hardy, Thomas, 1840–1928.
  [Poems. Selections]
  Hardy's selected poems / Thomas Hardy ; [editor, Bob Blaisdell].
     p.   cm. — (Dover thrift editions)
  Includes index.
  ISBN 0-486-28753-X (pbk.)
  I. Blaisdell, Robert. II. Title. III. Series
PR4742.B58   1995
821'.8 — dc20

95-19648
CIP

Manufactured in the United States of America
Dover Publications, Inc., 31 East 2nd Street, Mineola, N.Y. 11501

Note

THOMAS HARDY (1840–1928), author of several of the nineteenth century's great English novels (including *Tess of the D'Urbervilles*, *The Mayor of Casterbridge* and *Far from the Madding Crowd*), was also one of England's finest twentieth-century poets (all except his first volume of poems having been published after 1900). Hardy's writing career crossed centuries and genres, but he claimed to have always preferred writing poetry to novels. Several of his poems date from the 1860s, when he composed verses while an architecture student that he was to publish more than thirty years later. Though Hardy claimed to have given up novel-writing because of the poor critical reception of *Jude the Obscure* (1895), it is more likely that his financial success as a novelist had finally made his desired career as a poet possible.

Hardy's more than 900 poems are solid, fresh and finely crafted. His language has its roots in the full range of English — from literary idioms to folk dialects, archaic terms to neologisms, everyday expressions to technical words. This selection contains his strongest and most famous poems and demonstrates Hardy's full range of irony and tragedy, his inventiveness in poetic forms and his keen interest in folklore, current events and, in particular, memory. Death and love are favorite themes, from "Hap" (1866) to the last poems written in 1927. The death of his first wife, Emma, prompted the twenty-one "Poems of 1912–13," an especially poignant series about their courtship and marriage (a selection of these appear beginning on page 49 of this volume).

All but one of the sixty-nine poems in this selection come from the first edition of *Collected Poems of Thomas Hardy* (1919), which included the first five volumes of Hardy's verse (see Contents for titles and dates of the original volumes). Hardy went on to publish *Late Lyrics and Earlier* (1922), *Human Shows, Far Phantasies* (1925) and *Winter Words in Various Moods and Metres* (1928). He also wrote a three-part verse drama, *The Dynasts: A Drama of the Napoleonic Wars* (1903–08).

Contents

From *Time's Laughingstocks and Other Verses* (1909)

An uncollected poem (1911)

From *Satires of Circumstance* (1914)

From *Moments of Vision and Miscellaneous Verses* (1917)

Hap

If but some vengeful god would call to me
From up the sky, and laugh: 'Thou suffering thing,
Know that thy sorrow is my ecstasy,
That thy love's loss is my hate's profiting!'

Then would I bear it, clench myself, and die,
Steeled by the sense of ire unmerited;
Half-eased in that a Powerfuller than I
Had willed and meted me the tears I shed.

But not so. How arrives it joy lies slain,
And why unblooms the best hope ever sown?
—Crass Casualty obstructs the sun and rain,
And dicing[1] Time for gladness casts a moan. . . .
These purblind Doomsters had as readily strown
Blisses about my pilgrimage as pain.

1866

A Confession to a Friend in Trouble

Your troubles shrink not, though I feel them less
Here, far away, than when I tarried near;
I even smile old smiles—with listlessness—
Yet smiles they are, not ghastly mockeries mere.

A thought too strange to house within my brain
Haunting its outer precincts I discern:
—*That I will not show zeal again to learn
Your griefs, and, sharing them, renew my pain.* . . .

It goes, like murky bird or buccaneer
That shapes its lawless figure on the main,
And each new impulse tends to make outflee
The unseemly instinct that had lodgment here;

---

[1] *dicing*] dice-tossing.

1

Yet, comrade old, can bitterer knowledge be
Than that, though banned, such instinct was in me!

　1866

Neutral Tones

We stood by a pond that winter day,
And the sun was white, as though chidden of God,
And a few leaves lay on the starving sod;
　　　— They had fallen from an ash, and were gray.

Your eyes on me were as eyes that rove
Over tedious riddles solved years ago;
And some words played between us to and fro
　　　On which lost the more by our love.

The smile on your mouth was the deadest thing
Alive enough to have strength to die;
And a grin of bitterness swept thereby
　　　Like an ominous bird a-wing. . . .

Since then, keen lessons that love deceives,
And wrings with wrong, have shaped to me
Your face, and the God-curst sun, and a tree,
　　　And a pond edged with grayish leaves.

　1867

Her Initials

Upon a poet's page I wrote
Of old two letters of her name;
Part seemed she of the effulgent thought
Whence that high singer's rapture came.
— When now I turn the leaf the same
Immortal light illumes the lay,
But from the letters of her name
The radiance has waned away!

　1869

San Sebastian

(*August 1813*)

WITH THOUGHTS OF SERGEANT M—— (PENSIONER), WHO
· DIED 185–

'Why, Sergeant, stray on the Ivel Way,
As though at home there were spectres rife?
From first to last 'twas a proud career!
And your sunny years with a gracious wife
    Have brought you a daughter dear.

'I watched her to-day; a more comely maid,
As she danced in her muslin bowed with blue,
Round a Hintock maypole never gayed.'
—'Aye, aye; I watched her this day, too,
    As it happens,' the Sergeant said.

'My daughter is now,' he again began,
'Of just such an age as one I knew
When we of the Line, the Forlorn-hope van,
On an August morning—a chosen few—
    Stormed San Sebastian.

'She's a score less three; so about was *she*—
The maiden I wronged in Peninsular days. . . .
You may prate of your prowess in lusty times,
But as years gnaw inward you blink your bays,
    And see too well your crimes!

'We'd stormed it at night, by the flapping light
Of burning towers, and the mortar's boom:
We'd topped the breach; but had failed to stay,
For our files were misled by the baffling gloom;
    And we said we'd storm by day.

'So, out of the trenches, with features set,
On that hot, still morning, in measured pace,
Our column climbed; climbed higher yet,·
Passed the fauss'bray, scarp, up the curtain-face,
    And along the parapet.

'From the batteried hornwork the cannoneers
Hove crashing balls of iron fire;

On the shaking gap mount the volunteers
In files, and as they mount expire
    Amid curses, groans, and cheers.

'Five hours did we storm, five hours re-form,
As Death cooled those hot blood pricked on;
Till our cause was helped by a woe within:
They were blown from the summit we'd leapt upon,
    And madly we entered in.

'On end for plunder, 'mid rain and thunder
That burst with the lull of our cannonade,
We vamped the streets in the stifling air —
Our hunger unsoothed, our thirst unstayed —
    And ransacked the buildings there.

'From the shady vaults of their walls of white
We rolled rich puncheons of Spanish grape,
Till at length, with the fire of the wine alight,
I saw at a doorway a fair fresh shape —
    A woman, a sylph, or sprite.

'Afeard she fled, and with heated head
I pursued to the chamber she called her own;
—When might is right no qualms deter,
And having her helpless and alone
    I wreaked my will on her.

'She raised her beseeching eyes to me,
And I heard the words of prayer she sent
In her own soft language. . . . Fatefully
I copied those eyes for my punishment
    In begetting the girl you see!

'So, to-day I stand with a God-set brand
Like Cain's, when he wandered from kindred's ken. . . .
I served through the war that made Europe free;
I wived me in peace-year. But, hid from men,
    I bear that mark on me.

'Maybe we shape our offspring's guise
From fancy, or we know not what,
And that no deep impression dies, —
For the mother of my child is not
    The mother of her eyes.

'And I nightly stray on the Ivel Way
As though at home there were spectres rife;
I delight me not in my proud career;
And 'tis coals of fire that a gracious wife
    Should have brought me a daughter dear!'

The Burghers

(17 —)

The sun had wheeled from Grey's to Dammer's Crest,
And still I mused on that Thing imminent:
At length I sought the High-street to the West.

The level flare raked pane and pediment
And my wrecked face, and shaped my nearing friend
Like one of those the Furnace held unshent.

'I've news concerning her,' he said. 'Attend.
They fly to-night at the late moon's first gleam:
Watch with thy steel: two righteous thrusts will end

Her shameless visions and his passioned dream.
I'll watch with thee, to testify thy wrong —
To aid, maybe. — Law consecrates the scheme.'

I started, and we paced the flags along
Till I replied: 'Since it has come to this
I'll do it! But alone. I can be strong.'

Three hours past Curfew, when the Froom's mild hiss
Reigned sole, undulled by whirr of merchandize,
From Pummery-Tout to where the Gibbet is,

I crossed my pleasaunce hard by Glyd'path Rise,
And stood beneath the wall. Eleven strokes went,
And to the door they came, contrariwise,

And met in clasp so close I had but bent
My lifted blade on either to have let
Their two souls loose upon the firmament.

But something held my arm. 'A moment yet
As pray-time ere you wantons die!' I said;
And then they saw me. Swift her gaze was set

With eye and cry of love illimited
Upon her Heart-king. Never upon me
Had she thrown look of love so thoroughsped! . . .

At once she flung her faint form shieldingly
On his, against the vengeance of my vows;
The which o'erruling, her shape shielded he.

Blanked by such love, I stood as in a drowse,
And the slow moon edged from the upland nigh,
My sad thoughts moving thuswise: 'I may house

And I may husband her, yet what am I
But licensed tyrant to this bonded pair?
Says Charity, Do as ye would be done by.' . . .

Hurling my iron to the bushes there,
I bade them stay. And, as if brain and breast
Were passive, they walked with me to the stair.

Inside the house none watched; and on we prest
Before a mirror, in whose gleam I read
Her beauty, his, — and mine own mien unblest;

Till at her room I turned. 'Madam,' I said,
'Have you the wherewithal for this? Pray speak.
Love fills no cupboard. You'll need daily bread.'

'We've nothing, sire,' she lipped; 'and nothing seek.
'Twere base in me to rob my lord unware;
Our hands will earn a pittance week by week.'

And next I saw she had piled her raiment rare
Within the garde-robes, and her household purse,
Her jewels, her least lace of personal wear;

And stood in homespun. Now grown wholly hers,
I handed her the gold, her jewels all,
And him the choicest of her robes diverse.

'I'll take you to the doorway in the wall,
And then adieu,' I told them. 'Friends, withdraw.'
They did so; and she went — beyond recall.

And as I paused beneath the arch I saw
Their moonlit figures — slow, as in surprise —
Descend the slope, and vanish on the haw.

' "Fool," some will say,' I thought. — 'But who is wise,
Save God alone, to weigh my reasons why?'
— 'Hast thou struck home?' came with the boughs' night-sighs.

It was my friend. 'I have struck well. They fly,
But carry wounds that none can cicatrize.'
— 'Mortal?' said he. 'Remorseful — worse.'

Her Death and After

The summons was urgent: and forth I went —
By the way of the Western Wall, so drear
On that winter night, and sought a gate,
        Where one, by Fate,
    Lay dying that I held dear.

And there, as I paused by her tenement,
And the trees shed on me their rime and hoar,
I thought of the man who had left her lone —
        Him who made her his own
    When I loved her, long before.

The rooms within had the piteous shine
That home-things wear when there's aught amiss;
From the stairway floated the rise and fall
        Of an infant's call,
    Whose birth had brought her to this.

Her life was the price she would pay for that whine —
For a child by the man she did not love.
'But let that rest for ever,' I said,
        And bent my tread
    To the bedchamber above.

She took my hand in her thin white own,
And smiled her thanks — though nigh too weak —
And made them a sign to leave us there,
        Then faltered, ere
    She could bring herself to speak.

'Just to see you — before I go — he'll condone
Such a natural thing now my time's not much —

When Death is so near it hustles hence
        All passioned sense
Between woman and man as such!

'My husband is absent. As heretofore
The City detains him. But, in truth,
He has not been kind. . . . I will speak no blame,
        But—the child is lame;
    O, I pray she may reach his ruth!

'Forgive past days—I can say no more—
Maybe had we wed you would now repine! . . .
But I treated you ill. I was punished. Farewell!
        —Truth shall I tell?
    Would the child were yours and mine!

'As a wife I was true. But, such my unease
That, could I insert a deed back in Time,
I'd make her yours, to secure your care;
        And the scandal bear,
    And the penalty for the crime!'

—When I had left, and the swinging trees
Rang above me, as lauding her candid say,
Another was I. Her words were enough:
        Came smooth, came rough,
    I felt I could live my day.

Next night she died; and her obsequies
In the Field of Tombs where the earthworks frowned
Had her husband's heed. His tendance spent,
        I often went
    And pondered by her mound.

All that year and the next year whiled,
And I still went thitherward in the gloam;
But the Town forgot her and her nook,
        And her husband took
    Another Love to his home.

And the rumour flew that the lame lone child
Whom she wished for its safety child of mine,
Was treated ill when offspring came
        Of the new-made dame,
    And marked a more vigorous line.

A smarter grief within me wrought
Than even at loss of her so dear
That the being whose soul my soul suffused
      Had a child ill-used,
    While I dared not interfere!

One eve as I stood at my spot of thought
In the white-stoned Garth, brooding thus her wrong,
Her husband neared; and to shun his view
      By her hallowed mew
    I went from the tombs among

To the Cirque of the Gladiators which faced —
That haggard mark of Imperial Rome,
Whose Pagan echoes mock the chime
      Of our Christian time —
    And I drew to its bank and clomb.

The sun's gold touch was scarce displaced
From the vast Arena where men once bled,
When her husband followed; bowed; half-passed
      With lip upcast;
    Then halting sullenly said:

'It is noised that you visit my first wife's tomb.
Now, I gave her an honoured name to bear
While living, when dead. So I've claim to ask
      By what right you task
    My patience by vigiling there?

'There's decency even in death, I assume;
Preserve it, sir, and keep away;
For the mother of my first-born you
      Show mind undue!
    — Sir, I've nothing more to say.'

A desperate stroke discerned I then —
God pardon — or pardon not — the lie;
She had sighed that she wished (lest the child should pine
      Of slights) 'twere mine,
    So I said: 'But the father I.

'That you thought it yours is the way of men;
But I won her troth long ere your day:
You learnt how, in dying, she summoned me?

'Twas in fealty.
— Sir, I've nothing more to say,

'Save that, if you'll hand me my little maid,
I'll take her, and rear her, and spare you toil.
Think it more than a friendly act none can;
        I'm a lonely man,
    While you've a large pot to boil.

'If not, and you'll put it to ball or blade —
To-night, to-morrow night, anywhen —
I'll meet you here. . . . But think of it,
        And in season fit
    Let me hear from you again.'

— Well, I went away, hoping; but nought I heard
Of my stroke for the child, till there greeted me
A little voice that one day came
        To my window-frame
    And babbled innocently:

'My father who's not my own, sends word
I'm to stay here, sir, where I belong!'
Next a writing came: 'Since the child was the fruit
        Of your lawless suit,
    Pray take her, to right a wrong.'

And I did. And I gave the child my love,
And the child loved me, and estranged us none.
But compunctions loomed; for I'd harmed the dead
        By what I said
    For the good of the living one.

— Yet though, God wot, I am sinner enough,
And unworthy the woman who drew me so,
Perhaps this wrong for her darling's good
        She forgives, or would,
    If only she could know!

Her Immortality

Upon a noon I pilgrimed through
    A pasture, mile by mile,
Unto the place where last I saw
    My dead Love's living smile.

And sorrowing I lay me down
    Upon the heated sod:
It seemed as if my body pressed
    The very ground she trod.

I lay, and thought; and in a trance
    She came and stood thereby —
The same, even to the marvellous ray
    That used to light her eye.

'You draw me, and I come to you,
    My faithful one,' she said,
In voice that had the moving tone
    It bore ere breath had fled.

'Seven years have circled since I died:
    Few now remember me;
My husband clasps another bride:
    My children's love has she.

'My brethren, sisters, and my friends
    Care not to meet my sprite:
Who prized me most I did not know
    Till I passed down from sight.'

I said: 'My days are lonely here;
    I need thy smile alway:
I'll use this night my ball or blade,
    And join thee ere the day.'

A tremor stirred her tender lips,
    Which parted to dissuade:
'That cannot be, O friend,' she cried;
    'Think, I am but a Shade!

'A Shade but in its mindful ones
    Has immortality;

By living, me you keep alive,
    By dying you slay me.

'In you resides my single power
    Of sweet continuance here;
On your fidelity I count
    Through many a coming year.'

—I started through me at her plight,
    So suddenly confessed:
Dismissing late distaste for life,
    I craved its bleak unrest.

'I will not die, my One of all!—
    To lengthen out thy days
I'll guard me from minutest harms
    That may invest my ways!'

She smiled and went. Since then she comes
    Oft when her birth-moon climbs,
Or at the seasons' ingresses,
    Or anniversary times;

But grows my grief. When I surcease,
    Through whom alone lives she,
Her spirit ends its living lease,
    Never again to be!

Friends Beyond

William Dewy, Tranter Reuben, Farmer Ledlow[1] late at plough,
    Robert's kin, and John's, and Ned's,
And the Squire, and Lady Susan, lie in Mellstock churchyard now!

'Gone,' I call them, gone for good, that group of local hearts and
      heads;
    Yet at mothy curfew-tide,
And at midnight when the noon-heat breathes it back from walls
      and leads,

---

[1] *William Dewy, Tranter Reuben, Farmer Ledlow*] characters in one of Hardy's
early novels, *Under the Greenwood Tree* (1872).

They've a way of whispering to me — fellow-wight who yet abide —
    In the muted, measured note
Of a ripple under archways, or a lone cave's stillicide:[2]

'We have triumphed: this achievement turns the bane to antidote,
    Unsuccesses to success,
Many thought-worn eves and morrows to a morrow free of thought.

'No more need we corn and clothing, feel of old terrestial stress;
    Chill detraction stirs no sigh;
Fear of death has even bygone us: death gave all that we possess.'

W.D. — 'Ye mid burn the old bass-viol that I set such value by.'
Squire. — 'You may hold the manse in fee,
    You may wed my spouse, may let my children's memory of me
      die.'

Lady S. — 'You may have my rich brocades, my laces; take each
    household key;
    Ransack coffer, desk, bureau;
    Quiz the few poor treasures hid there, con the letters kept by
      me.'

Far. — 'Ye mid zell my favourite heifer, ye mid let the charlock[3]
    grow,
    Foul the grinterns,[4] give up thrift.'
Far. Wife. — 'If ye break my best blue china, children, I shan't care
    or ho.'

All. — 'We've no wish to hear the tidings, how the people's fortunes
    shift;
    What your daily doings are;
    Who are wedded, born, divided; if your lives beat slow or swift.

'Curious not the least are we if our intents you make or mar,
    If you quire to our old tune,
If the City stage still passes, if the weirs still roar afar.'

— Thus, with very gods' composure, freed those crosses late and
    soon
    Which, in life, the Trine allow
(Why, none witteth), and ignoring all that haps beneath the moon,

---

[2] *stillicide*] dripping.
[3] *charlock*] a weed.
[4] *grinterns*] granary bins.

William Dewy, Tranter Reuben, Farmer Ledlow late at plough,
    Robert's kin, and John's, and Ned's,
And the Squire, and Lady Susan, murmur mildly to me now.

Nature's Questioning

When I look forth at dawning, pool,
    Field, flock, and lonely tree,
    All seem to gaze at me
Like chastened children sitting silent in a school;

Their faces dulled, constrained, and worn,
    As though the master's ways
    Through the long teaching days
Had cowed them till their early zest was overborne.

Upon them stirs in lippings mere
    (As if once clear in call,
    But now scarce breathed at all)—
'We wonder, ever wonder, why we find us here!

'Has some Vast Imbecility,
    Mighty to build and blend,
    But impotent to tend,
Framed us in jest, and left us now to hazardry?

'Or come we of an Automaton
    Unconscious of our pains? . . .
    Or are we live remains
Of Godhead dying downwards, brain and eye now gone?

'Or is it that some high Plan betides,
    As yet not understood,
    Of Evil stormed by Good,
We the Forlorn Hope over which Achievement strides?'

Thus things around. No answerer I. . . .
    Meanwhile the winds, and rains,
    And Earth's old glooms and pains
Are still the same, and Death and glad Life neighbour nigh.

I Look into My Glass

I look into my glass,
And view my wasting skin,
And say, 'Would God it came to pass
My heart had shrunk as thin!'

For then, I, undistrest
By hearts grown cold to me,
Could lonely wait my endless rest
With equanimity.

But Time, to make me grieve,
Part steals, lets part abide;
And shakes this fragile frame at eve
With throbbings of noontide.

The Going of the Battery

Wives' Lament
(2 November 1899)

I

O it was sad enough, weak enough, mad enough —
Light in their loving as soldiers can be —
First to risk choosing them, leave alone losing them
Now, in far battle, beyond the South Sea! . . .

II

— Rain came down drenchingly; but we unblenchingly
Trudged on beside them through mirk and through mire,
They stepping steadily — only too readily! —
Scarce as if stepping brought parting-time nigher.

III

Great guns were gleaming there, living things seeming there,
Cloaked in their tar-cloths, upmouthed to the night;
Wheels wet and yellow from axle to felloe,
Throats blank of sound, but prophetic to sight.

IV

Gas-glimmers drearily, blearily, eerily
Lit our pale faces outstretched for one kiss,
While we stood prest to them, with a last quest to them
Not to court perils that honour could miss.

V

Sharp were those sighs of ours, blinded these eyes of ours,
When at last moved away under the arch
All we loved. Aid for them each woman prayed for them,
Treading back slowly the track of their march.

VI

Some one said: 'Nevermore will they come: evermore
Are they now lost to us.' O it was wrong!
Though may be hard their ways, some Hand will guard their ways,
Bear them through safely, in brief time or long.

VII

— Yet, voices haunting us, daunting us, taunting us,
Hint in the night-time when life beats are low
Other and graver things. . . . Hold we to braver things,
Wait we, in trust, what Time's fulness shall show.

Drummer Hodge[1]

I

They throw in Drummer Hodge, to rest
      Uncoffined — just as found:
His landmark is a kopje-crest[2]
      That breaks the veldt around:
And foreign constellations west
      Each night above his mound.

---

[1] *Drummer Hodge*] a John Doe from Wessex who fought in the Boer War (1899–1902) in South Africa.
[2] *kopje-crest*] hilltop.

II

Young Hodge the Drummer never knew—
      Fresh from his Wessex home—
The meaning of the broad Karoo,[3]
      The Bush, the dusty loam,
And why uprose to nightly view
      Strange stars amid the gloam.

III

Yet portion of that unknown plain
      Will Hodge for ever be;
His homely Northern breast and brain
      Grow to some Southern tree,
And strange-eyed constellations reign
      His stars eternally.

The Souls of the Slain

I

      The thick lids of Night closed upon me
            Alone at the Bill
            Of the Isle by the Race—
      Many-caverned, bald, wrinkled of face—
And with darkness and silence the spirit was on me
            To brood and be still.

II

      No wind fanned the flats of the ocean,
            Or promontory sides,
            Or the ooze by the strand,
      Or the bent-bearded slope of the land,
Whose base took its rest amid everlong motion
            Of criss-crossing tides.

III

      Soon from out of the Southward seemed nearing
            A whirr, as of wings
            Waved by mighty-vanned flies,

---

[3] *Karoo*] a high, dry plateau in South Africa.

Or by night-moths of measureless size,
And in softness and smoothness well-nigh beyond hearing
Of corporal things.

IV

And they bore to the bluff, and alighted —
A dim-discerned train
Of sprites without mould,
Frameless souls none might touch or might hold —
On the ledge by the turreted lantern, far-sighted
By men of the main.

V

And I heard them say 'Home!' and I knew them
For souls of the felled
On the earth's nether bord
Under Capricorn, whither they'd warred,
And I neared in my awe, and gave heedfulness to them
With breathings inheld.

VI

Then, it seemed, there approached from the northward
A senior soul-flame
Of the like filmy hue:
And he met them and spake: 'Is it you,
O my men?' Said they, 'Aye! We bear homeward and hearthward
To feast on our fame!'

VII

'I've flown there before you,' he said then:
'Your households are well;
But — your kin linger less
On your glory and war-mightiness
Than on dearer things.' — 'Dearer?' cried these from the dead then,
'Of what do they tell?'

VIII

'Some mothers muse sadly, and murmur
Your doings as boys —
Recall the quaint ways
Of your babyhood's innocent days.
Some pray that, ere dying, your faith had grown firmer,
And higher your joys.

IX

    'A father broods: "Would I had set him
        To some humble trade,
        And so slacked his high fire,
    And his passionate martial desire;
And told him no stories to woo him and whet him
        To this dire crusade!" '

X

    'And, General, how hold out our sweethearts,
        Sworn loyal as doves?'
        — 'Many mourn; many think
    It is not unattractive to prink
Them in sables for heroes. Some fickle and fleet hearts
        Have found them new loves.'

XI

    'And our wives?' quoth another resignedly,
        'Dwell they on our deeds?'
        — 'Deeds of home; that live yet
    Fresh as new — deeds of fondness or fret;
Ancient words that were kindly expressed or unkindly,
        These, these have their heeds.'

XII

    — 'Alas! then it seems that our glory
        Weighs less in their thought
        Than our old homely acts,
    And the long-ago commonplace facts
Of our lives — held by us as scarce part of our story,
        And rated as nought!'

XIII

    Then bitterly some: 'Was it wise now
        To raise the tomb-door
        For such knowledge? Away!'
    But the rest: 'Fame we prized till to-day;
Yet that hearts keep us green for old kindness we prize now
        A thousand times more!'

XIV

    Thus speaking, the trooped apparitions
        Began to disband

And resolve them in two:
Those whose record was lovely and true
Bore to northward for home: those of bitter traditions
        Again left the land,

XV

And, towering to seaward in legions,
        They paused at a spot
        Overbending the Race —
That engulphing, ghast, sinister place —
Whither headlong they plunged, to the fathomless regions
        Of myriads forgot.

XVI

And the spirits of those who were homing
        Passed on, rushingly,
        Like the Pentecost Wind;
And the whirr of their wayfaring thinned
And surceased on the sky, and but left in the gloaming
        Sea-mutterings and me.

    December 1899

Rome
The Vatican: Sala delle Muse

(*1887*)

I sat in the Muses' Hall at the mid of the day,
And it seemed to grow still, and the people to pass away,
And the chiselled shapes to combine in a haze of sun,
Till beside a Carrara column there gleamed forth One.

She looked not this nor that of those beings divine,
But each and the whole — an essence of all the Nine;
With tentative foot she neared to my halting-place,
A pensive smile on her sweet, small, marvellous face.

'Regarded so long, we render thee sad?' said she.
'Not you,' sighed I, 'but my own inconstancy!
I worship each and each; in the morning one,
And then, alas! another at sink of sun.

'To-day my soul clasps Form; but where is my troth
Of yesternight with Tune: can one cleave to both?'
— 'Be not perturbed,' said she. 'Though apart in fame,
As I and my sisters are one, those, too, are the same.'

— 'But my love goes further — to Story, and Dance, and Hymn,
The lover of all in a sun-sweep is fool to whim —
Is swayed like a river-weed as the ripples run!'
— 'Nay, wight, thou sway'st not. These are but phases of one;

'And that one is I; and I am projected from thee,
One that out of thy brain and heart thou causest to be —
Extern to thee nothing. Grieve not, nor thyself becall,
Woo where thou wilt; and rejoice thou canst love at all!'

A Commonplace Day

The day is turning ghost,
And scuttles from the kalendar in fits and furtively,
To join the anonymous host
Of those that throng oblivion; ceding his place, maybe,
To one of like degree.

I part the fire-gnawed logs,
Rake forth the embers, spoil the busy flames, and lay the ends
Upon the shining dogs;[1]
Further and further from the nooks the twilight's stride extends,
And beamless black impends.

Nothing of tiniest worth
Have I wrought, pondered, planned; no one thing asking blame or
praise,
Since the pale corpse-like birth
Of this diurnal unit, bearing blanks in all its rays —
Dullest of dull-hued Days!

Wanly upon the panes
The rain slides, as have slid since morn my colourless thoughts;
and yet
Here, while Day's presence wanes,
And over him the sepulchre-lid is slowly lowered and set,
He wakens my regret.

---

[1] *dogs*] the metal supports for logs in a fireplace.

Regret — though nothing dear
That I wot[2] of, was toward in the wide world at his prime,
Or bloomed elsewhere than here,
To die with his decease, and leave a memory sweet, sublime,
Or mark him out in Time. . . .

—Yet, maybe, in some soul,
In some spot undiscerned on sea or land, some impulse rose,
Or some intent upstole
Of that enkindling ardency from whose maturer glows
The world's amendment flows;

But which, benumbed at birth
By momentary chance or wile, has missed its hope to be
Embodied on the earth;
And undervoicings of this loss to man's futurity
May wake regret in me.

Doom and She

I

There dwells a mighty pair —
Slow, statuesque, intense —
Amid the vague Immense:
None can their chronicle declare,
Nor why they be, nor whence.

II

Mother of all things made,
Matchless in artistry,
Unlit with sight is she. —
And though her ever well-obeyed
Vacant of feeling he.

III

The Matron mildly asks —
A throb in every word —
'Our clay-made creatures, lord,

---

[2] *wot*] know.

How fare they in their mortal tasks
    Upon Earth's bounded bord?

IV

    'The fate of those I bear,
    Dear lord, pray turn and view,
    And notify me true;
Shapings that eyelessly I dare
    Maybe I would undo.

V

    'Sometimes from lairs of life
    Methinks I catch a groan,
    Or multitudinous moan,
As though I had schemed a world of strife,
    Working by touch alone.'

VI

    'World-weaver!' he replies,
    'I scan all thy domain;
    But since nor joy nor pain
It lies in me to recognize,
    I read thy realms in vain.

VII

    'World-weaver! what *is* Grief?
    And what are Right, and Wrong,
    And Feeling, that belong
To creatures all who owe thee fief?
    Why is Weak worse than Strong?' . . .

VIII

    So, baffled, curious, meek,
    She broods in sad surmise. . . .
    — Some say they have heard her sighs
On Alpine height or Polar peak
    When the night tempests rise.

The Subalterns

I

'Poor wanderer,' said the leaden sky,
      'I fain would lighten thee,
But there are laws in force on high
      Which say it must not be.'

II

— 'I would not freeze thee, shorn one,' cried
      The North, 'knew I but how
To warm my breath, to slack my stride;
      But I am ruled as thou.'

III

— 'To-morrow I attack thee, wight,'
      Said Sickness. 'Yet I swear
I bear thy little ark no spite,
      But am bid enter there.'

IV

— 'Come hither, Son,' I heard Death say;
      'I did not will a grave
Should end thy pilgrimage to-day,
      But I, too, am a slave!'

V

We smiled upon each other then,
      And life to me wore less
Of that fell guise it wore ere when
      They owned their passiveness.

His Immortality

I

      I saw a dead man's finer part
Shining within each faithful heart
Of those bereft. Then said I: 'This must be
            His immortality.'

II

     I looked there as the seasons wore,
And still his soul continuously bore
A life in theirs. But less its shine excelled
        Than when I first beheld.

III

     His fellow-yearsmen passed, and then
In later hearts I looked for him again;
And found him — shrunk, alas! into a thin
        And spectral mannikin.

IV

     Lastly I ask — now old and chill —
If aught of him remain unperished still;
And find, in me alone, a feeble spark,
        Dying amid the dark.

   February 1899

An August Midnight

I

A shaded lamp and a waving blind,
And the beat of a clock from a distant floor:
On this scene enter — winged, horned, and spined —
A longlegs, a moth, and a dumbledore;[1]
While 'mid my page there idly stands
A sleepy fly, that rubs its hands. . . .

II

Thus meet we five, in this still place,
At this point of time, at this point in space.
— My guests besmear my new-penned line,
Or bang at the lamp and fall supine.
'God's humblest, they!' I muse. Yet why?
They know Earth-secrets that know not I.

   Max Gate, 1899

---

[1] *dumbledore*] bumblebee.

The Darkling Thrush

I leant upon a coppice gate
    When Frost was spectre-gray,
And Winter's dregs made desolate
    The weakening eye of day.
The tangled bine-stems scored the sky
    Like strings from broken lyres,
And all mankind that haunted nigh
    Had sought their household fires.

The land's sharp features seemed to be
    The Century's corpse outleant,
His crypt the cloudy canopy,
    The wind his death-lament.
The ancient pulse of germ and birth
    Was shrunken hard and dry,
And every spirit upon earth
    Seemed fervourless as I.

At once a voice burst forth among
    The bleak twigs overhead
In a full-hearted evensong
    Of joy illimited;
An aged thrush, frail, gaunt, and small,
    In blast-beruffled plume,
Had chosen thus to fling his soul
    Upon the growing gloom.

So little cause for carollings
    Of such ecstatic sound
Was written on terrestrial things
    Afar or nigh around,
That I could think there trembled through
    His happy good-night air
Some blessed Hope, whereof he knew
    And I was unaware.

December 1900

A Wasted Illness

Through vaults of pain,
Enribbed and wrought with groins of ghastliness,
I passed, and garish spectres moved my brain
　　　　To dire distress.

And hammerings,
And quakes, and shoots, and stifling hotness, blent
With webby waxing things and waning things
　　　　As on I went.

'Where lies the end
To this foul way?' I asked with weakening breath.
Thereon ahead I saw a door extend—
　　　　The door to Death.

It loomed more clear:
'At last!' I cried. 'The all-delivering door!'
And then, I knew not how, it grew less near
　　　　Than theretofore.

And back slid I
Along the galleries by which I came,
And tediously the day returned, and sky,
　　　　And life—the same.

And all was well:
Old circumstance resumed its former show,
And on my head the dews of comfort fell
　　　　As ere my woe.

I roam anew,
Scarce conscious of my late distress. . . . And yet
Those backward steps to strength I cannot view
　　　　Without regret.

For that dire train
Of waxing shapes and waning, passed before,
And those grim chambers, must be ranged again
　　　　To reach that door.

A Man

(In Memory of H. of M.)

I

In Casterbridge there stood a noble pile,
Wrought with pilaster, bay, and balustrade
In tactful times when shrewd Eliza swayed. —
        On burgher, squire, and clown
It smiled the long street down for near a mile.

II

But evil days beset that domicile;
The stately beauties of its roof and wall
Passed into sordid hands. Condemned to fall
        Were cornice, quoin, and cove,
And all that art had wove in antique style.

III

Among the hired dismantlers entered there
One till the moment of his task untold.
When charged therewith he gazed, and answered bold:
        'Be needy I or no,
I will not help lay low a house so fair!

IV

'Hunger is hard. But since the terms be such —
No wage, or labour stained with the disgrace
Of wrecking what our age cannot replace
        To save its tasteless soul —
I'll do without your dole. Life is not much!'

V

Dismissed with sneers he backed his tools and went,
And wandered workless; for it seemed unwise
To close with one who dared to criticize
        And carp on points of taste:
Rude men should work where placed, and be content.

VI

Years whiled. He aged, sank, sickened; and was not:
And it was said, 'A man intractable

And curst is gone.' None sighed to hear his knell,
     None sought his churchyard-place;
His name, his rugged face, were soon forgot.

VII

The stones of that fair hall lie far and wide,
And but a few recall its ancient mould;
Yet when I pass the spot I long to hold
     As truth what fancy saith:
'His protest lives where deathless things abide!'

The Levelled Churchyard

'O Passenger, pray list and catch
     Our sighs and piteous groans,
Half stifled in this jumbled patch
     Of wrenched memorial stones!

'We late-lamented, resting here,
     Are mixed to human jam,
And each to each exclaims in fear,
     "I know not which I am!"

'The wicked people have annexed
     The verses on the good;
A roaring drunkard sports the text
     Teetotal Tommy should!

'Where we are huddled none can trace,
     And if our names remain,
They pave some path or porch or place
     Where we have never lain!

'Here's not a modest maiden elf
     But dreads the final Trumpet,
Lest half of her should rise herself,
     And half some local strumpet!

'From restorations of Thy fane,
     From smoothings of Thy sward,
From zealous Churchmen's pick and plane
     Deliver us O Lord! Amen!'

1882

The Ruined Maid

'O 'Melia, my dear, this does everything crown!
Who could have supposed I should meet you in Town?
And whence such fair garments, such prosperi-ty?' —
'O didn't you know I'd been ruined?' said she.

— 'You left us in tatters, without shoes or socks,
Tired of digging potatoes, and spudding up docks;
And now you've gay bracelets and bright feathers three!' —
'Yes: that's how we dress when we're ruined,' said she.

— 'At home in the barton[1] you said "thee" and "thou",
And "thik oon", and "theäs oon", and "t'other"; but now
Your talking quite fits 'ee for high compa-ny!' —
'Some polish is gained with one's ruin,' said she.

— 'Your hands were like paws then, your face blue and bleak
But now I'm bewitched by your delicate cheek,
And your little gloves fit as on any la-dy!' —
'We never do work when we're ruined,' said she.

— 'You used to call home-life a hag-ridden dream,
And you'd sigh, and you'd sock; but at present you seem
To know not of megrims or melancho-ly!' —
'True. One's pretty lively when ruined,' said she.

— 'I wish I had feathers, a fine sweeping gown,
And a delicate face, and could strut about Town!' —
'My dear — a raw country girl, such as you be,
Cannot quite expect that. You ain't ruined,' said she.

Westbourne Park Villas, 1866

---

[1] *barton*] farmyard.

In Tenebris[1] I

'Percussus sum sicut fœnum, et aruit cor meum.'—Ps. CI[2]

Wintertime nighs;
But my bereavement-pain
It cannot bring again:
Twice no one dies.

Flower-petals flee;
But, since it once hath been,
No more that severing scene
Can harrow me.

Birds faint in dread:
I shall not lose old strength
In the lone frost's black length:
Strength long since fled!

Leaves freeze to dun;
But friends can not turn cold
This season as of old
For him with none.

Tempests may scath;
But love can not make smart
Again this year his heart
Who no heart hath.

Black is night's cope;
But death will not appal
One who, past doubtings all,
Waits in unhope.

---

[1] *In Tenebris*] Latin for "In Darkness."
[2] *'Percussus . . . meum.'*] Latin for "My heart is smitten, and withered like grass" (from Psalm 102 in the King James Bible; Hardy's reference is to the Vulgate).

In Tenebris II

'Considerabam ad dexteram, et videbam; et non erat qui cognosceret
    me. . . . non est qui requirat animam meam.'—Ps. CXLI [1]

When the clouds' swoln bosoms echo back the shouts of the many
    and strong
That things are all as they best may be, save a few to be right ere
    long,
And my eyes have not the vision in them to discern what to these is
    so clear,
The blot seems straightway in me alone; one better he were not
    here.

The stout upstanders say, All's well with us: ruers have nought to
    rue!
And what the potent say so oft, can it fail to be somewhat true?
Breezily go they, breezily come; their dust smokes around their
    career,
Till I think I am one born out of due time, who has no calling here.

Their dawns bring lusty joys, it seems; their eves exultance sweet;
Our times are blessed times, they cry: Life shapes it as is most meet,
And nothing is much the matter; there are many smiles to a tear;
Then what is the matter is I, I say. Why should such an one be
    here? . . .

Let him to whose ears the low-voiced Best seems stilled by the clash
    of the First,
Who holds that if way to the Better there be, it exacts a full look at
    the Worst,
Who feels that delight is a delicate growth cramped by crooked-
    ness, custom, and fear,
Get him up and be gone as one shaped awry; he disturbs the order
    here.

    1895–96

---

[1] *'Considerabam . . . meam.'*] Latin for "I looked on my right hand, and beheld,
but there was no man that would know me: . . . no man cared for my soul" (from
Psalm 142 in the King James Bible).

In Tenebris III

'Heu mihi, quia incolatus meus prolongatus est! Habitavi cum habitan-
tibus Cedar. Multum incola fuit anima mea.'—Ps. CXIX[1]

There have been times when I well might have passed and the
    ending have come —
Points in my path when the dark might have stolen on me, artless,
    unrueing —
Ere I had learnt that the world was a welter of futile doing:
Such had been times when I well might have passed, and the
    ending have come!

Say, on the noon when the half-sunny hours told that April was
    nigh,
And I upgathered and cast forth the snow from the crocus-border,
Fashioned and furbished the soil into a summer-seeming order,
Glowing in gladsome faith that I quickened the year thereby.

Or on that loneliest of eves when afar and benighted we stood,
She who upheld me and I, in the midmost of Egdon together,
Confident I in her watching and ward through the blackening
    heather,
Deeming her matchless in might and with measureless scope
    endued.

Or on that winter-wild night when, reclined by the chimney-nook
    quoin,
Slowly a drowse overgat me, the smallest and feeblest of folk there,
Weak from my baptism of pain; when at times and anon I awoke
    there —
Heard of a world wheeling on, with no listing or longing to join.

Even then! while unweeting[2] that vision could vex or that knowl-
    edge could numb,
That sweets to the mouth in the belly are bitter, and tart, and
    untoward,

---

[1] *'Heu . . . mea.'*] Latin for "Woe to me that I sojourn in Mesech, that I dwell in
the tents of Kedar. My soul hath long dwelt with him that hateth peace" (from
Psalm 120 in the King James Bible).
[2] *unweeting*] not knowing.

Then, on some dim-coloured scene should my briefly raised cur-
    tain have lowered,
Then might the Voice that is law have said 'Cease!' and the ending
    have come.

1896

Tess's Lament

I

I would that folk forgot me quite,
                Forgot me quite!
I would that I could shrink from sight,
        And no more see the sun.
Would it were time to say farewell,
To claim my nook, to need my knell,
Time for them all to stand and tell
        Of my day's work as done.

II

Ah! dairy where I lived so long,
                I lived so long;
Where I would rise up staunch and strong,
        And lie down hopefully.
'Twas there within the chimney-seat
He watched me to the clock's slow beat —
Loved me, and learnt to call me Sweet,
        And whispered words to me.

III

And now he's gone; and now he's gone; . . .
                And now he's gone!
The flowers we potted perhaps are thrown
        To rot upon the farm.
And where we had our supper-fire
May now grow nettle, dock, and briar,
And all the place be mould and mire
        So cozy once and warm.

IV

And it was I who did it all,
                    Who did it all;
'Twas I who made the blow to fall
        On him who thought no guile.
Well, it is finished — past, and he
Has left me to my misery,
And I must take my Cross on me
        For wronging him awhile.

V

How gay we looked that day we wed,
                    That day we wed!
'May joy be with ye!' they all said
        A-standing by the durn.[1]
I wonder what they say o'us now,
And if they know my lot; and how
She feels who milks my favourite cow,
        And takes my place at churn!

VI

It wears me out to think of it,
                    To think of it;
I cannot bear my fate as writ,
        I'd have my life unbe;
Would turn my memory to a blot,
Make every relic of me rot,
My doings be as they were not,
        And gone all trace of me!

Bereft

    In the black winter morning
No light will be struck near my eyes
While the clock in the stairway is warning
For five, when he used to rise.
                Leave the door unbarred,

---

[1] *durn*] doorposts.

The clock unwound,
Make my lone bed hard —
Would 'twere underground!

When the summer dawns clearly,
And the appletree-tops seem alight,
Who will undraw the curtain and cheerly
Call out that the morning is bright?

When I tarry at market
No form will cross Durnover Lea
In the gathering darkness, to hark at
Grey's Bridge for the pit-pat o' me.

When the supper crock's steaming,
And the time is the time of his tread,
I shall sit by the fire and wait dreaming
In a silence as of the dead.
Leave the door unbarred,
The clock unwound,
Make my lone bed hard —
Would 'twere underground!

1901

Shut Out That Moon

Close up the casement, draw the blind,
    Shut out that stealing moon,
She wears too much the guise she wore
    Before our lutes were strewn
With years-deep dust, and names we read
    On a white stone were hewn.

Step not out on the dew-dashed lawn
    To view the Lady's Chair,
Immense Orion's glittering form,
    The Less and Greater Bear:
Stay in; to such sights we were drawn
    When faded ones were fair.

Brush not the bough for midnight scents
    That come forth lingeringly,
And wake the same sweet sentiments
    They breathed to you and me
When living seemed a laugh, and love
    All it was said to be.

Within the common lamp-lit room
    Prison my eyes and thought;
Let dingy details crudely loom,
    Mechanic speech be wrought:
Too fragrant was Life's early bloom,
    Too tart the fruit it brought!

    1904

The Night of the Dance

The cold moon hangs to the sky by its horn,
    And centres its gaze on me;
The stars, like eyes in reverie,
Their westering as for a while forborne,
    Quiz downward curiously.

Old Robert draws the backbrand in,
    The green logs steam and spit;
The half-awakened sparrows flit
From the riddled thatch; and owls begin
    To whoo from the gable-slit.

Yes; far and nigh things seem to know
    Sweet scenes are impending here;
That all is prepared; that the hour is near
For welcomes, fellowships, and flow
    Of sally, song, and cheer;

That spigots are pulled and viols strung;
    That soon will arise the sound
Of measures trod to tunes renowned;
That She will return in Love's low tongue
    My vows as we wheel around.

Julie-Jane

Sing; how 'a would sing!
How 'a would raise the tune
When we rode in the waggon from harvesting
    By the light o' the moon!

Dance; how 'a would dance!
If a fiddlestring did but sound
She would hold out her coats, give a slanting glance,
    And go round and round.

Laugh; how 'a would laugh!
Her peony lips would part
As if none such a place for a lover to quaff
    At the deeps of a heart.

Julie, O girl of joy,
Soon, soon that lover he came.
Ah, yes; and gave thee a baby-boy,
    But never his name. . . .

— Tolling for her, as you guess;
And the baby too. . . . 'Tis well.
You knew her in maidhood likewise? — Yes,
    That's her burial bell.

'I suppose,' with a laugh, she said,
'I should blush that I'm not a wife;
But how can it matter, so soon to be dead,
    What one does in life!'

When we sat making the mourning
By her death-bed side, said she,
'Dears, how can you keep from your lovers, adorning
    In honour of me!'

Bubbling and brightsome eyed!
But now — O never again.
She chose her bearers before she died
    From her fancy-men.

A Church Romance

(*Mellstock: circa 1835*)

She turned in the high pew, until her sight
Swept the west gallery, and caught its row
Of music-men with viol, book, and bow
Against the sinking sad tower-window light.

She turned again; and in her pride's despite
One strenuous viol's inspirer seemed to throw
A message from his string to her below,
Which said: 'I claim thee as my own forthright!'

Thus their hearts' bond began, in due time signed.
And long years thence, when Age had scared Romance,
At some old attitude of his or glance
That gallery-scene would break upon her mind,
With him as minstrel, ardent, young, and trim,
Bowing 'New Sabbath' or 'Mount Ephraim'.

The Rambler

I do not see the hills around,
Nor mark the tints the copses wear;
I do not note the grassy ground
And constellated daisies there.

I hear not the contralto note
Of cuckoos hid on either hand,
The whirr that shakes the nighthawk's throat
When eve's brown awning hoods the land.

Some say each songster, tree, and mead —
All eloquent of love divine —
Receives their constant careful heed:
Such keen appraisement is not mine.

The tones around me that I hear,
The aspects, meanings, shapes I see,
Are those far back ones missed when near,
And now perceived too late by me!

A Wet Night

I pace along, the rain-shafts riddling me,
Mile after mile out by the moorland way,
And up the hill, and through the ewe-leaze[1] gray
Into the lane, and round the corner tree;

Where, as my clothing clams me, mire-bestarred,
And the enfeebled light dies out of day,
Leaving the liquid shades to reign, I say,
'This is a hardship to be calendared!'

Yet sires of mine now perished and forgot,
When worse beset, ere roads were shapen here,
And night and storm were foes indeed to fear,
Times numberless have trudged across this spot
In sturdy muteness on their strenuous lot,
And taking all such toils as trifles mere.

God's Education

I saw him steal the light away
    That haunted in her eye:
It went so gently none could say
More than that it was there one day
    And missing by-and-by.

I watched her longer, and he stole
    Her lily tincts and rose;
All her young sprightliness of soul
Next fell beneath his cold control,
    And disappeared like those.

I asked: 'Why do you serve her so?
    Do you, for some glad day,
Hoard these her sweets — ?' He said, 'O no,
They charm not me; I bid Time throw
    Them carelessly away.'

---

[1] *ewe-leaze*] sheep-pasture.

Said I: 'We call that cruelty —
 We, your poor mortal kind.'
He mused. 'The thought is new to me.
Forsooth, though I men's master be,
 Theirs is the teaching mind!'

The Man He Killed

 'Had he and I but met
 By some old ancient inn,
We should have sat us down to wet
 Right many a nipperkin![1]

 'But ranged as infantry,
 And staring face to face,
I shot at him as he at me,
 And killed him in his place.

 'I shot him dead because —
 Because he was my foe,
Just so: my foe of course he was;
 That's clear enough; although

 'He thought he'd 'list, perhaps,
 Off-hand like — just as I —
Was out of work — had sold his traps —
 No other reason why.

 'Yes; quaint and curious war is!
 You shoot a fellow down
You'd treat if met where any bar is,
 Or help to half-a-crown.'

 1902

---

[1] *nipperkin*] a shot of liquor.

The Calf[1]

You may have seen, in road or street
    At times, when passing by,
A creature with bewildered bleat
Behind a milcher's tail, whose feet
    Went pit-pat. That was I.

Whether we are of Devon kind,
    Shorthorns, or Herefords,
We are in general of one mind
That in the human race we find
    Our masters and our lords.

When grown up (if they let me live)
    And in a dairy-home,
I may less wonder and misgive
Than now, and get contemplative,
    And never wish to roam.

And in some fair stream, taking sips,
    May stand through summer noons,
With water dribbling from my lips
And rising halfway to my hips,
    And babbling pleasant tunes.

Channel Firing

That night your great guns, unawares,
Shook all our coffins as we lay,
And broke the chancel window-squares,
We thought it was the Judgment-day

And sat upright. While drearisome
Arose the howl of wakened hounds:
The mouse let fall the altar-crumb,
The worms drew back into the mounds,

---

[1] Hardy wrote this for *The Book of Baby Beasts* (1911) by Florence Dugdale; she became his second wife in 1914.

The glebe cow drooled. Till God called, 'No;
It's gunnery practice out at sea
Just as before you went below;
The world is as it used to be:

'All nations striving strong to make
Red war yet redder. Mad as hatters
They do no more for Christés sake
Than you who are helpless in such matters.

'That this is not the judgment-hour
For some of them's a blessed thing,
For if it were they'd have to scour
Hell's floor for so much threatening. . . .

'Ha, ha. It will be warmer when
I blow the trumpet (if indeed
I ever do; for you are men,
And rest eternal sorely need).'

So down we lay again. 'I wonder,
Will the world ever saner be,'
Said one, 'than when He sent us under
In our indifferent century!'

And many a skeleton shook his head.
'Instead of preaching forty year,'
My neighbour Parson Thirdly said,
'I wish I had stuck to pipes and beer.'

Again the guns disturbed the hour,
Roaring their readiness to avenge,
As far inland as Stourton Tower,
And Camelot, and starlit Stonehenge.

April 1914

The Convergence of the Twain

(*Lines on the loss of the 'Titanic'*)

I

In a solitude of the sea
Deep from human vanity,
And the Pride of Life that planned her, stilly couches she.

II

Steel chambers, late the pyres
Of her salamandrine fires,
Cold currents thrid, and turn to rhythmic tidal lyres.

III

Over the mirrors meant
To glass the opulent
The sea-worm crawls — grotesque, slimed, dumb, indifferent.

IV

Jewels in joy designed
To ravish the sensuous mind
Lie lightless, all their sparkles bleared and black and blind.

V

Dim moon-eyed fishes near
Gaze at the gilded gear
And query: 'What does this vaingloriousness down here?' . . .

VI

Well: while was fashioning
This creature of cleaving wing,
The Immanent Will that stirs and urges everything

VII

Prepared a sinister mate
For her — so gaily great —
A Shape of Ice, for the time far and dissociate.

VIII

　　　And as the smart ship grew
　　　In stature, grace, and hue,
In shadowy silent distance grew the Iceberg too.

IX

　　　Alien they seemed to be:
　　　No mortal eye could see
The intimate welding of their later history,

X

　　　Or sign that they were bent
　　　By paths coincident
On being anon twin halves of one august event,

XI

　　　Till the Spinner of the Years
　　　Said 'Now!' And each one hears,
And consummation comes, and jars two hemispheres.

Beyond the Last Lamp

(*Near Tooting Common*)

I

While rain, with eve in partnership,
Descended darkly, drip, drip, drip,
Beyond the last lone lamp I passed
　　Walking slowly, whispering sadly,
　　Two linked loiterers, wan, downcast:
Some heavy thought constrained each face,
And blinded them to time and place.

II

The pair seemed lovers, yet absorbed
In mental scenes no longer orbed
By love's young rays. Each countenance
　　As it slowly, as it sadly
　　Caught the lamplight's yellow glance,
Held in suspense a misery
At things which had been or might be.

III

When I retrod that watery way
Some hours beyond the droop of day,
Still I found pacing there the twain
  Just as slowly, just as sadly,
  Heedless of the night and rain.
One could but wonder who they were,
And what wild woe detained them there.

IV

Though thirty years of blur and blot
Have slid since I beheld that spot,
And saw in curious converse there
  Moving slowly, moving sadly
  That mysterious tragic pair,
Its olden look may linger on —
All but the couple; they have gone.

V

Whither? Who knows, indeed. . . . And yet
To me, when nights are weird and wet,
Without those comrades there at tryst
  Creeping slowly, creeping sadly,
  That lone lane does not exist.
There they seem brooding on their pain,
And will, while such a lane remain.

The Face at the Casement

  If ever joy leave
An abiding sting of sorrow,
So befell it on the morrow
  Of that May eve. . . .

  The travelled sun dropped
To the north-west, low and lower,
The pony's trot grew slower,
  Until we stopped.

  'This cosy house just by
I must call at for a minute,

A sick man lies within it
    Who soon will die.

    'He wished to — marry me,
So I am bound, when I drive near him,
To inquire, if but to cheer him,
    How he may be.'

    A message was sent in,
And wordlessly we waited,
Till some one came and stated
    The bulletin.

    And that the sufferer said,
For her call no words could thank her;
As his angel he must rank her
    Till life's spark fled.

    Slowly we drove away,
When I turned my head, although not
Called to: why I turned I know not
    Even to this day:

    And lo, there in my view
Pressed against an upper lattice
Was a white face, gazing at us
    As we withdrew.

    And well did I divine
It to be the man's there dying,
Who but lately had been sighing
    For her pledged mine.

    Then I deigned a deed of hell;
It was done before I knew it;
What devil made me do it
    I cannot tell!

    Yes, while he gazed above,
I put my arm about her
That he might see, nor doubt her
    My plighted Love.

    The pale face vanished quick,
As if blasted, from the casement,
And my shame and self-abasement
    Began their prick.

And they prick on, ceaselessly,
For that stab in Love's fierce fashion
Which, unfired by lover's passion,
    Was foreign to me.

She smiled at my caress,
But why came the soft embowment
Of her shoulder at that moment
    She did not guess.

Long long years has he lain
In thy garth, O sad Saint Cleather:
What tears there, bared to weather,
    Will cleanse that stain!

Love is long-suffering, brave,
Sweet, prompt, precious as a jewel;
But O, too, Love is cruel,
    Cruel as the grave.

Ah, Are You Digging on My Grave?

'Ah, are you digging on my grave
    My loved one? — planting rue?'
— 'No: yesterday he went to wed
One of the brightest wealth has bred.
"It cannot hurt her now," he said,
    "That I should not be true." '

'Then who is digging on my grave?
    My nearest dearest kin?'
— 'Ah, no: they sit and think, "What use!
What good will planting flowers produce?
No tendance of her mound can loose
    Her spirit from Death's gin." '

'But some one digs upon my grave?
    My enemy? — prodding sly?'
— 'Nay: when she heard you had passed the Gate
That shuts on all flesh soon or late,
She thought you no more worth her hate,
    And cares not where you lie.'

'Then, who is digging on my grave?
    Say — since I have not guessed!'
— 'O it is I, my mistress dear,
Your little dog, who still lives near,
And much I hope my movements here
    Have not disturbed your rest?'

'Ah, yes! *You* dig upon my grave. . . .
    Why flashed it not on me
That one true heart was left behind!
What feeling do we ever find
To equal among human kind
    A dog's fidelity!'

'Mistress, I dug upon your grave
    To bury a bone, in case
I should be hungry near this spot
When passing on my daily trot.
I am sorry, but I quite forgot
    It was your resting-place.'

The Going[1]

Why did you give no hint that night
That quickly after the morrow's dawn,
And calmly, as if indifferent quite,
You would close your term here, up and be gone
    Where I could not follow
    With wing of swallow
To gain one glimpse of you ever anon!

    Never to bid good-bye,
    Or lip me the softest call,
Or utter a wish for a word, while I
Saw morning harden upon the wall,
    Unmoved, unknowing
    That your great going
Had place that moment, and altered all.

---

[1] This poem and the five poems that follow, through "The Phantom Horse-woman," are from the series "Poems of 1912–13," reflective verses on the recent death of Emma Hardy, the poet's first wife.

Why do you make me leave the house
And think for a breath it is you I see
At the end of the alley of bending boughs
Where so often at dusk you used to be;
  Till in darkening dankness
  The yawning blankness
Of the perspective sickens me!

  You were she who abode
  By those red-veined rocks far West,
You were the swan-necked one who rode
Along the beetling Beeny Crest,
  And, reining nigh me,
  Would muse and eye me,
While Life unrolled us its very best.

Why, then, latterly did we not speak,
Did we not think of those days long dead,
And ere your vanishing strive to seek
That time's renewal? We might have said,
  'In this bright spring weather
  We'll visit together
Those places that once we visited.'

  Well, well! All's past amend,
  Unchangeable. It must go.
I seem but a dead man held on end
To sink down soon. . . . O you could not know
  That such swift fleeing
  No soul foreseeing —
Not even I — would undo me so!

  December 1912

I Found Her Out There

I found her out there
On a slope few see,
That falls westwardly
To the salt-edged air,
Where the ocean breaks
On the purple strand,

And the hurricane shakes
The solid land.

I brought her here,
And have laid her to rest
In a noiseless nest
No sea beats near.
She will never be stirred
In her loamy cell
By the waves long heard
And loved so well.

So she does not sleep
By those haunted heights
The Atlantic smites
And the blind gales sweep,
Whence she often would gaze
At Dundagel's famed head,
While the dipping blaze
Dyed her face fire-red;

And would sigh at the tale
Of sunk Lyonnesse,
As a wind-tugged tress
Flapped her cheek like a flail;
Or listen at whiles
With a thought-bound brow
To the murmuring miles
She is far from now.

Yet her shade, maybe,
Will creep underground
Till it catch the sound
Of that western sea
As it swells and sobs
Where she once domiciled,
And joy in its throbs
With the heart of a child.

The Haunter

He does not think that I haunt here nightly:
　　How shall I let him know
That whither his fancy sets him wandering
　　I, too, alertly go? —
Hover and hover a few feet from him
　　Just as I used to do,
But cannot answer the words he lifts me —
　　Only listen thereto!

When I could answer he did not say them:
　　When I could let him know
How I would like to join in his journeys
　　Seldom he wished to go.
Now that he goes and wants me with him
　　More than he used to do,
Never he sees my faithful phantom
　　Though he speaks thereto.

Yes, I companion him to places
　　Only dreamers know,
Where the shy hares print long paces,
　　Where the night rooks go;
Into old aisles where the past is all to him,
　　Close as his shade can do,
Always lacking the power to call to him,
　　Near as I reach thereto!

What a good haunter I am, O tell him!
　　Quickly make him know
If he but sigh since my loss befell him
　　Straight to his side I go.
Tell him a faithful one is doing
　　All that love can do
Still that his path may be worth pursuing,
　　And to bring peace thereto.

The Voice

Woman much missed, how you call to me, call to me,
Saying that now you are not as you were
When you had changed from the one who was all to me,
But as at first, when our day was fair.

Can it be you that I hear? Let me view you, then,
Standing as when I drew near to the town
Where you would wait for me: yes, as I knew you then,
Even to the original air-blue gown!

Or is it only the breeze, in its listlessness
Travelling across the wet mead to me here,
You being ever dissolved to existlessness,
Heard no more again far or near?

Thus I; faltering forward,
Leaves around me falling,
Wind oozing thin through the thorn from norward,
And the woman calling.

December 1912

At Castle Boterel

As I drive to the junction of lane and highway,
And the drizzle bedrenches the waggonette,
I look behind at the fading byway,
And see on its slope, now glistening wet,
Distinctly yet

Myself and a girlish form benighted
In dry March weather. We climb the road
Beside a chaise. We had just alighted
To ease the sturdy pony's load
When he sighed and slowed.

What we did as we climbed, and what we talked of
Matters not much, nor to what it led, —
Something that life will not be balked of

Without rude reason till hope is dead,
    And feeling fled.

It filled but a minute. But was there ever
    A time of such quality, since or before,
In that hill's story? To one mind never,
    Though it has been climbed, foot-swift, foot-sore,
        By thousands more.

Primaeval rocks form the road's steep border,
    And much have they faced there, first and last,
Of the transitory in Earth's long order;
    But what they record in colour and cast
        Is — that we two passed.

And to me, though Time's unflinching rigour,
    In mindless rote, has ruled from sight
The substance now, one phantom figure
    Remains on the slope, as when that night
        Saw us alight.

I look and see it there, shrinking, shrinking,
    I look back at it amid the rain
For the very last time; for my sand is sinking,
    And I shall traverse old love's domain
        Never again.

March 1913

The Phantom Horsewoman

I

Queer are the ways of a man I know:
        He comes and stands
        In a careworn craze,
        And looks at the sands
        And the seaward haze
        With moveless hands
        And face and gaze,
        Then turns to go . . .
And what does he see when he gazes so?

II

They say he sees as an instant thing
        More clear than to-day,
        A sweet soft scene
        That once was in play
        By that briny green;
        Yes, notes alway
        Warm, real, and keen,
        What his back years bring —
A phantom of his own figuring.

III

Of this vision of his they might say more:
        Not only there
        Does he see this sight,
        But everywhere
        In his brain — day, night,
        As if on the air
        It were drawn rose-bright —
        Yea, far from that shore
Does he carry this vision of heretofore:

IV

A ghost-girl-rider. And though, toil-tried,
        He withers daily,
        Time touches her not,
        But she still rides gaily
        In his rapt thought
        On that shagged and shaly
        Atlantic spot,
        And as when first eyed
Draws rein and sings to the swing of the tide.

1913

The Moth-Signal

(*On Egdon Heath*)

'What are you still, still thinking,'
    He asked in vague surmise,
'That you stare at the wick unblinking
    With those deep lost luminous eyes?'

'O, I see a poor moth burning
    In the candle flame,' said she,
'Its wings and legs are turning
    To a cinder rapidly.'

'Moths fly in from the heather,'
    He said, 'now the days decline.'
'I know,' said she. 'The weather,
    I hope, will at last be fine.

'I think,' she added lightly,
    'I'll look out at the door.
The ring the moon wears nightly
    May be visible now no more.'

She rose, and, little heeding,
    Her life-mate then went on
With his mute museful reading
    In the annals of ages gone.

Outside the house a figure
    Came from the tumulus near,
And speedily waxed bigger,
    And clasped and called her Dear.

'I saw the pale-winged token
    You sent through the crack,' sighed she.
'That moth is burnt and broken
    With which you lured out me.

'And were I as the moth is
    It might be better far
For one whose marriage troth is
    Shattered as potsherds are!'

Then grinned the Ancient Briton
   From the tumulus treed with pine:
'So, hearts are thwartly smitten
   In these days as in mine!'

The Death of Regret

I opened my shutter at sunrise,
   And looked at the hill hard by,
And I heartily grieved for the comrade
   Who wandered up there to die.

I let in the morn on the morrow,
   And failed not to think of him then,
As he trod up that rise in the twilight,
   And never came down again.

I undid the shutter a week thence,
   But not until after I'd turned
Did I call back his last departure
   By the upland there discerned.

Uncovering the casement long later,
   I bent to my toil till the gray,
When I said to myself, 'Ah — what ails me,
   To forget him all the day!'

As daily I flung back the shutter
   In the same blank bald routine,
He scarcely once rose to remembrance
   Through a month of my facing the scene.

And ah, seldom now do I ponder
   At the window as heretofore
On the long valued one who died yonder,
   And wastes by the sycamore.

Exeunt Omnes[1]

I

      Everybody else, then, going,
And I still left where the fair was? . . .
Much have I seen of neighbour loungers
      Making a lusty showing,
      Each now past all knowing.

II

      There is an air of blankness
In the street and the littered spaces;
Thoroughfare, steeple, bridge and highway
      Wizen themselves to lankness;
      Kennels dribble dankness.

III

      Folk all fade. And whither,
As I wait alone where the fair was?
Into the clammy and numbing night-fog
      Whence they entered hither.
      Soon do I follow thither!

   2 June 1913

We Sat at the Window

(*Bournemouth, 1875*)

We sat at the window looking out,
And the rain came down like silken strings
That Swithin's day. Each gutter and spout
Babbled unchecked in the busy way
      Of witless things:
Nothing to read, nothing to see
Seemed in that room for her and me
      On Swithin's day.

---

[1] *Exeunt Omnes*] theatrical term for the exit of all characters from the stage.

We were irked by the scene, by our own selves; yes,
For I did not know, nor did she infer
How much there was to read and guess
By her in me, and to see and crown
    By me in her.
Wasted were two souls in their prime,
And great was the waste, that July time
    When the rain came down.

Afternoon Service at Mellstock

(*Circa 1850*)

    On afternoons of drowsy calm
      We stood in the panelled pew,
Singing one-voiced a Tate-and-Brady psalm
      To the tune of 'Cambridge New'.

    We watched the elms, we watched the rooks,
      The clouds upon the breeze,
Between the whiles of glancing at our books,
      And swaying like the trees.

    So mindless were those outpourings! —
      Though I am not aware
That I have gained by subtle thought on things
      Since we stood psalming there.

To My Father's Violin

    Does he want you down there
    In the Nether Glooms where
The hours may be a dragging load upon him,
      As he hears the axle grind
        Round and round
      Of the great world, in the blind
        Still profound
Of the night-time? He might liven at the sound
Of your string, revealing you had not forgone him.

In the gallery west the nave,
But a few yards from his grave,
Did you, tucked beneath his chin, to his bowing
    Guide the homely harmony
        Of the quire
    Who for long years strenuously —
        Son and sire —
Caught the strains that at his fingering low or higher
From your four thin threads and eff-holes came outflowing.

And, too, what merry tunes
He would bow at nights or noons
That chanced to find him bent to lute a measure,
    When he made you speak his heart
        As in dream,
    Without book or music-chart,
        On some theme
Elusive as a jack-o'-lanthorn's gleam,
And the psalm of duty shelved for trill of pleasure.

Well, you cannot, alas,
The barrier overpass
That screens him in those Mournful Meads hereunder,
    Where no fiddling can be heard
        In the glades
    Of silentness, no bird
        Thrills the shades;
Where no viol is touched for songs or serenades,
No bowing wakes a congregation's wonder.

He must do without you now,
Stir you no more anyhow
To yearning concords taught you in your glory;
    While, your strings a tangled wreck,
        Once smart drawn,
    Ten worm-wounds in your neck,
        Purflings wan
With dust-hoar, here alone I sadly con
Your present dumbness, shape your olden story.

1916

The Pedigree

I

I bent in the deep of night
Over a pedigree the chronicler gave
As mine; and as I bent there, half-unrobed,
The uncurtained panes of my window-square let in the watery light
Of the moon in its old age:
And green-rheumed clouds were hurrying past where mute and
cold it globed
Like a drifting dolphin's eye seen through a lapping wave.

II

So, scanning my sire-sown tree,
And the hieroglyphs of this spouse tied to that,
With offspring mapped below in lineage,
Till the tangles troubled me,
The branches seemed to twist into a scared and cynic face
Which winked and tokened towards the window like a Mage
Enchanting me to gaze again thereat.

III

It was a mirror now,
And in it a long perspective I could trace
Of my begetters, dwindling backward each past each
All with the kindred look,
Whose names had since been inked down in their place
On the recorder's book,
Generation and generation of my mien, and build, and brow.

IV

And then did I divine
That every heave and coil and move I made
Within my brain, and in my mood and speech,
Was in the glass portrayed
As long forestalled by their so making it;
The first of them, the primest fuglemen of my line,
Being fogged in far antiqueness past surmise and reason's reach.

V

Said I then, sunk in tone,
'I am merest mimicker and counterfeit! —
Though thinking, *I am I,*
And what I do I do myself alone.'
—The cynic twist of the page thereat unknit
Back to its normal figure, having wrought its purport wry,
The Mage's mirror left the window-square,
And the stained moon and drift retook their places there.

1916

The Oxen

Christmas Eve, and twelve of the clock.
'Now they are all on their knees,'
An elder said as we sat in a flock
By the embers in hearthside ease.

We pictured the meek mild creatures where
They dwelt in their strawy pen,
Nor did it occur to one of us there
To doubt they were kneeling then.

So fair a fancy few would weave
In these years! Yet, I feel,
If someone said on Christmas Eve,
'Come; see the oxen kneel

'In the lonely barton by yonder coomb[1]
Our childhood used to know,'
I should go with him in the gloom,
Hoping it might be so.

1915

---

[1] *coomb*] valley.

Transformations

Portion of this yew
Is a man my grandsire knew,
Bosomed here at its foot:
This branch may be his wife,
A ruddy human life
Now turned to a green shoot.

These grasses must be made
Of her who often prayed,
Last century, for repose;
And the fair girl long ago
Whom I often tried to know
May be entering this rose.

So, they are not underground,
But as nerves and veins abound
In the growths of upper air,
And they feel the sun and rain,
And the energy again
That made them what they were!

Great Things

Sweet cyder is a great thing,
    A great thing to me,
Spinning down to Weymouth town
    By Ridgway thirstily,
And maid and mistress summoning
    Who tend the hostelry:
O cyder is a great thing,
    A great thing to me!

The dance it is a great thing,
    A great thing to me,
With candles lit and partners fit
    For night-long revelry;
And going home when day-dawning
    Peeps pale upon the lea:

O dancing is a great thing,
    A great thing to me!

Love is, yea, a great thing,
    A great thing to me,
When, having drawn across the lawn
    In darkness silently,
A figure flits like one a-wing
    Out from the nearest tree:
O love is, yes, a great thing,
    Aye, greatest thing to me!

Will these be always great things,
    Greatest things to me? . . .
Let it befall that One will call,
    'Soul, I have need of thee:'
What then? Joy-jaunts, impassioned flings,
    Love, and its ecstasy,
Will always have been great things,
    Greatest things to me!

Overlooking the River Stour

The swallows flew in the curves of an eight
        Above the river-gleam
        In the wet June's last beam:
Like little crossbows animate
The swallows flew in the curves of an eight
        Above the river-gleam.

Planing up shavings of crystal spray
        A moor-hen darted out
        From the bank thereabout,
And through the stream-shine ripped his way;
Planing up shavings of crystal spray
        A moor-hen darted out.

Closed were the kingcups; and the mead
        Dripped in monotonous green,
        Though the day's morning sheen
Had shown it golden and honeybee'd;
Closed were the kingcups; and the mead
        Dripped in monotonous green.

And never I turned my head, alack,
> While these things met my gaze
> Through the pane's drop-drenched glaze,
To see the more behind my back. . . .
O never I turned, but let, alack,
> These less things hold my gaze!

During Wind and Rain

> They sing their dearest songs —
> He, she, all of them — yea,
> Treble and tenor and bass,
>> And one to play;
> With the candles mooning each face. . . .
>> Ah, no; the years O!
How the sick leaves reel down in throngs!

> They clear the creeping moss —
> Elders and juniors — aye,
> Making the pathways neat
>> And the garden gay;
> And they build a shady seat. . . .
>> Ah, no; the years, the years;
See, the webbed white storm-birds wing across.

> They are blithely breakfasting all —
> Men and maidens — yea,
> Under the summer tree,
>> With a glimpse of the bay,
> While pet fowl come to the knee. . . .
>> Ah, no; the years O!
And the rotten rose is ript from the wall.

> They change to a high new house,
> He, she, all of them — aye,
> Clocks and carpets and chairs
>> On the lawn all day,
> And brightest things that are theirs. . . .
>> Ah, no; the years, the years;
Down their chiselled names the rain-drop ploughs.

Who's in the Next Room?

'Who's in the next room? — who?
    I seemed to see
Somebody in the dawning passing through,
        Unknown to me.'
'Nay: you saw nought. He passed invisibly.'

'Who's in the next room? — who?
    I seem to hear
Somebody muttering firm in a language new
        That chills the ear.'
'No: you catch not his tongue who has entered there.'

'Who's in the next room? — who?
    I seem to feel
His breath like a clammy draught, as if it drew
        From the Polar Wheel.'
'No: none who breathes at all does the door conceal.'

'Who's in the next room? — who?
    A figure wan
With a message to one in there of something due?
        Shall I know him anon?'
'Yea he; and he brought such; and you'll know him anon.'

The Masked Face

I found me in a great surging space,
    At either end a door,
And I said: 'What is this giddying place,
    With no firm-fixéd floor,
    That I knew not of before?'
    'It is Life,' said a mask-clad face.

I asked: 'But how do I come here,
    Who never wished to come;

Can the light and air be made more clear,
  The floor more quietsome,
  And the doors set wide? They numb
  Fast-locked, and fill with fear.'

The mask put on a bleak smile then,
  And said, 'O vassal-wight,
There once complained a goosequill pen
  To the scribe of the Infinite
  Of the words it had to write
  Because they were past its ken.'

The Clock of the Years

'A spirit passed before my face; the hair of my flesh stood up.'[1]

  And the Spirit said,
'I can make the clock of the years go backward,
But am loth to stop it where you will.'
  And I cried, 'Agreed
  To that. Proceed:
  It's better than dead!'

  He answered, 'Peace;'
And called her up — as last before me;
Then younger, younger she freshed, to the year
  I first had known
  Her woman-grown,
  And I cried, 'Cease! —

  'Thus far is good —
It is enough — let her stay thus always!'
But alas for me — He shook his head:
  No stop was there;
  And she waned child-fair,
  And to babyhood.

  Still less in mien
To my great sorrow became she slowly,

---

[1] 'A *spirit . . . up.*'] from Job 4:15.

And smalled till she was nought at all
   In his checkless griff;
   And it was as if
   She had never been.

   'Better,' I plained,
'She were dead as before! The memory of her
Had lived in me; but it cannot now!'
   And coldly his voice:
   'It was your choice
   To mar the ordained.'

 1916

The Shadow on the Stone

  I went by the Druid stone
 That broods in the garden white and lone,
And I stopped and looked at the shifting shadows
 That at some moments there are thrown
 From the tree hard by with a rhythmic swing,
 And they shaped in my imagining
To the shade that a well-known head and shoulders
 Threw there when she was gardening.

  I thought her behind my back,
 Yea, her I long had learned to lack,
And I said: 'I am sure you are standing behind me,
 Though how do you get into this old track?'
 And there was no sound but the fall of a leaf
 As a sad response; and to keep down grief
I would not turn my head to discover
 That there was nothing in my belief.

  Yet I wanted to look and see
 That nobody stood at the back of me;
But I thought once more: 'Nay, I'll not unvision
 A shape which, somehow, there may be.'
 So I went on softly from the glade,
 And left her behind me throwing her shade,
As she were indeed an apparition —
 My head unturned lest my dream should fade.

 Begun 1913: finished 1916

An Upbraiding

Now I am dead you sing to me
    The songs we used to know,
But while I lived you had no wish
    Or care for doing so.

Now I am dead you come to me
    In the moonlight, comfortless;
Ah, what would I have given alive
    To win such tenderness!

When you are dead, and stand to me
    Not differenced, as now,
But like again, will you be cold
    As when we lived, or how?

In Time of 'The Breaking of Nations'[1]

I

Only a man harrowing clods
    In a slow silent walk
With an old horse that stumbles and nods
    Half asleep as they stalk.

II

Only thin smoke without flame
    From the heaps of couch-grass;
Yet this will go onward the same
    Though Dynasties pass.

III

Yonder a maid and her wight
    Come whispering by:
War's annals will cloud into night
    Ere their story die.

1915

---

[1] Jer., LI 20. [Hardy's note.]

Afterwards

When the Present has latched its postern behind my tremulous
    stay,
    And the May month flaps its glad green leaves like wings,
Delicate-filmed as new-spun silk, will the neighbours say,
    'He was a man who used to notice such things'?

If it be in the dusk when, like an eyelid's soundless blink,
    The dewfall-hawk comes crossing the shades to alight
Upon the wind-warped upland thorn, a gazer may think,
    'To him this must have been a familiar sight.'

If I pass during some nocturnal blackness, mothy and warm,
    When the hedgehog travels furtively over the lawn,
One may say, 'He strove that such innocent creatures should come
    to no harm,
    But he could do little for them; and now he is gone.'

If, when hearing that I have been stilled at last, they stand at the
    door,
    Watching the full-starred heavens that winter sees,
Will this thought rise on those who will meet my face no more,
    'He was one who had an eye for such mysteries'?

And will any say when my bell of quittance is heard in the gloom,
    And a crossing breeze cuts a pause in its outrollings,
Till they rise again, as they were a new bell's boom,
    'He hears it not now, but used to notice such things'?

Alphabetical List of Titles

Alphabetical List of First Lines